# ORDINARY TIME

# ORDINARY TIME

Joseph P. Clancy

First Impression—2000

ISBN 1 85902 739 3

This book is published with the support of the
Arts Council of Wales.

Printed in Wales at
Gomer Press, Llandysul, Ceredigion

# CONTENTS

CONTENTS (*continued*)

# I. DAYS OF GRACE

## ADVENT 1993

There should be darkness
There should be silence
Admission of emptiness
Expectation
Of light and music.

We have lost all patience
We have trimmed the tree
Our streets are brilliant
With coloured lights
Our shops are loud with carols
Weeks before His coming
We have had our fill of Christmas.

But there on our TV screens
Between the mirth and the adverts
Is the silence
Is the darkness
In the skeleton limbs of children
In mothers' vacant eyes
In the charred flesh of families
On the cold hearths of their homes,

And we turn away and stare
Through the tinsel and the lights
Silently into the stubborn dark
Of the human heart
Crying out of its emptiness
For the coming of the Child.

## THE GIVEN TIME

From sister, daughters, neighbour, milkman, friend,
Six calendars this Christmas, hazarding
A year's worth of our future. I could wish
All years now a recurrence of these last.

It seems ridiculous, in our late sixties,
Vexed with arthritic limbs, abbreviated breaths,
That this should be the good time—these years, a
                                    honeymoon.
But oh, to stop the clocks! to stay this age forever!

Late afternoon. At the top of the hill, a grove
Ripe with October sunlight. Here we will linger,
Grateful, while we may. From me, this year, a wristwatch,
To tell how dear these moments as they pass.

# AT GETTYSBURG

1.  Alien as a spacecraft from some distant galaxy,
    This platform on its metal struts commands
    A view of ridges, woodlands, meadows,
    The nine roads where two armies dustily
    Converged, upon what was
    An ordinary country town.

    The roads are paved now, lined
    With guest-house and antique shop.
    The town's chief business
    Is to display its scars.

    Ascend the Observation Tower. Overlook
    The battlefield, the cemetery.
    Like the hundred-thirty years between
    That time and ours, it serves to keep
    History at a distance.

2.  Row after row of cannon
    Define the empty fields. The car,
    As though we made the Stations of the Cross,
    Proceeds from monument to monument,
    Site to site,
    Tracing the three-day transfiguration
    Of farmland into battleground.

    Wheatfield. Peach Orchard. June
    Sunlight is a blessing. We cannot feel
    The blaze of their July. We cannot
    Hear the rebel yell, the screams. We cannot
    See the smoke, the tumbling bodies. We cannot
    Smell the rotting flesh. We cannot taste
    The third day's evening rain.

3. The visitors in shorts and T-shirts
   Stroll amid tidy files of gravestones
   And underneath the ancient trees.

   The purple beech is gnarled, contorted.
   The tulip poplar's straight and tall.

4. *A flat failure*, Lincoln said. The words
   Would outlive the occasion. Whatever

   Those buried here believed they fought for,
   They died for his idea. Antithesis and metaphor

   Articulate a meaning for the place.
   From blood and bones, disintegrating flesh,

   He forged a sacred text, incorporated here
   An American sanctum. In that benediction

   A future was determined. This
   Is no place for deconstruction.

## OLD WOMAN

At ease in August sunlight and sea air,
She sits upon the bench, and watches gulls

Riding the breeze and tide-swell. Her hands
Are too arthritic now for knitting.

She nods and smiles politely as we pass.
She does not welcome those who stop to chat.

Nothing to say. Nothing to do.
Two years ago, she burned the photographs,

Album by album. Here and now
Suffices. Being; content to be.

THE GRAVE
*for Pat Geiringer*

Side by side, like headboards for twin beds,
These white rectangular stones at the far end of the
                                        churchyard.

On his, the name, the dates of birth and death.
On hers, the name, the date of birth.

Her health is good. It may be twenty years
Before an unknown hand confirms

Her affirmation of their life together. She stops by
Some days, in driving back from town,

With flowers. She attends
A different church most Sundays.

This grave her past, her future. She knows
She has been loved. She loves.

Whatever faith says will be true hereafter,
She is assured of a reunion here.

# DEATH NOTICES

Today, as every day, they've died
*Peacefully, in hospital,*
Or *Suddenly, at home.*

Does no one in this country die
Suddenly in hospital,
Or peacefully at home?

My mother died, six years ago,
Suddenly, at home.
We found her lying, in the early morning,
On the floor beside her bed,
Mouth gaping, like a fish on ice,
Eyes staring—in bewilderment? in terror?
At what? At what?

My father died some twenty years before,
Not suddenly, not peacefully, in hospital.
His urine-poisoned flesh refused
A patient dying. For weeks, with wrists and ankles
Bound to the bed-frame,
He tossed upon his cross, and cried out
*Margaret...Margaret...Margaret.*

Not my mother's name. She waited hours
Each day to hear it.
*Margaret...Margaret...Margaret.*
His older sister, who had cared for him in boyhood.

Watching my father die,
Not peacefully, not suddenly,
My mother died in hospital,
Long years before she died at home.

15

REBIRTH

*for our grandson Zachary, born deaf and with a defective heart, after his recovery at fifteen from a sudden collapse into coma*

It was as though we saw you in the womb.
You seemed to float upon your bed, unknowing,
Sustained by tubes and wires.

Your eyes opened. Everything was new
And nameless. You had to learn
To read the silent world again.

You knew us. Fumbled to sign our names.
We lived again
The fifteen-year-old joy of your first birth.

Yet it was not the same.
This time we knew, and loved in our rejoicing,
Who was being born.

# A BACKWARD LOOK

*for Kellie, Tommy, and Ben in Houston, Texas*

Once upon a far-off time, before
Soft rock, hard rock, punk rock, heavy metal,
Between ragtime and rhythm-and-blues,
An age without transistors, Walkmans, ghetto-blasters,
Before FM, before TV,
In that post-war, pre-nuclear epoch of your grandparents'
                                         growing-up,
Each home had just one radio.

And in the evening, after the children's programs,
*Jack Armstrong, Little Orphan Annie, Uncle Don,*
All of us, old and middle-aged and young,
Before teenagers had been invented,
Would gather in the living-room and listen
To the same music,
Live broadcasts of big bands from hotel ballrooms,
Kern and Gershwin, Rodgers, Porter, and Berlin.

Was it a better time, a better music?
Seventy is tempted to tell Sixteen it was
And hear within this blare that jars our ears
The fragmentation of society.

And yet, and yet,
Better to bite our tongues, be thankful
For what good was in our past,
And trust there's goodness in your tribal racket
We cannot hope or wish to comprehend.

17

## BULL'S EYE

A dog's eye will grow warm with affection,
gleam playfully,

a cat's, though aloof and alien,
scan analytically,

but this is wholly other,
incomprehensible,

in the half-dark of the byre
rolls meltingly in our direction,

passive, bewildered,
reflecting nothing of our human selves,

innocent.

# THE COPULATION OF THE ANIMALS

They are mindless of the camera's intrusion.
They are not driven

To protect their privacy. They will not be tempted
To watch themselves perform.

They cannot simulate behaviour. They are not
Politically correct.

She submits. He mounts her from the rear.
Joyless conjunction. They obey the naked

Dictates of their season. They discover
To the viewer voyeur the determination

Of genes to reproduce themselves. They
Are finished products. They cannot tell us

What to make of our programmes.

# HERON MUSIC

There is air and water in it. The angularity
Of stiff legs slowly striding, wading slowly
Through the shallows. Stillness in it. The sinuosity
Of neck poised over ripples, waiting, waiting.

There is solitude in it. The singular concentration
Of eyes upon fish. Severity in it. Suddenness:
Neck a shaft, beak splitting the brook. There is
Economy in it. Precision. Satisfaction.

There is gravity in it. The stability, year after year,
Of the bracken-lined bowl of sticks in the tall tree.
Serenity in it, of wings weighing the wind
Ruffling feathers, whistling through trailing toes.

CRUCIFIX
*The Catholic Chaplaincy, Edinburgh University*

Suspended from the ceiling on thin chains, aslant,
It hovers high above the altar.
As though from a trapeze, He hangs
By hands and feet, suspended
Into time, diverting
From prayer and homily.

Ascending, or descending?
We gaze beyond the Host now raised to Him
In consecration. Time suspended, we await
The swing of the trapeze.

# CHRISTMAS MARKET, LINCOLN

No different, perhaps, than centuries ago:
A slow surge through the cobbled streets,
Up Steep Hill, into Castle Square.

Somewhere beyond the screen of heads and shoulders
A silver band plays carols. Clowns, a carousel,
The smell of roasting pork. Pedestrian

Gridlock at every corner. The cram of bodies
Clogs progress through the sweet stalls, dish stalls, stalls
Of dolls and toys, of candles, baubles, pots.

Not even the cathedral can afford
Sanctuary from the crush of flesh.
Like grains of sand our queue streams through

Its simulacrum of eternity. Up the north aisle,
Into the Great Transept, where cross-beams from
Dean's Eye and Bishop's Eye transfix

The radiant elevation of a Christmas tree
Before the rood-screen. Then to Saint Hugh's Choir.
In the Angel Choir beyond, the Lincoln Imp

Grins in the twilight over Saint Hugh's Head
And the staring transients. We process
Past Katherine Swynford's chantry, underneath

The vaulting Gothic ribs, and press
Into the shop where the cathedral too
Is marketing Christmas. Tree trimmings, souvenir

Tea towels, trinkets of the Lincoln Imp.
Some shoppers here and there about the nave
Have slipped into a chair. They may remain

For evensong. A few, about to leave,
Will pause and linger by the sculpted figures
Of Nativity. Arrested in mid-stride

Two boyish shepherds gaze aloft,
Attending an unseen annunciation.
Three breathless elders peek through cracks

In a stable wall, confounded by
The young Jewish mother, sprawled full-length
Upon her elbows, smiling in delighted

Contemplation of her laughing baby.
Her husband, prone upon the stable floor,
Head cradled in his folded arms, is dreaming

Of children slaughtered in the world without
The walls of stable and cathedral calling
For the advent of the Child.

# TOWARDS THE MILLENNIUM

Won't someone tell them, please, they've got it wrong?
Jesus was born, the scholars say, six years before
Zero A. D. Commemoration is already
Out of date.

The Pope envisions, nonetheless, a year of grace,
Pan-Christian conclaves in Jerusalem and Bethlehem,
A gathering of Christian, Muslim, Jew on Sinai
To pray for peace.

Post-Christians, too, will celebrate the Year 2000
(C. E., of course). Those who live by other stories
Will ignore it: they have other numbers
For marking time.

Time's something more, though, than our fabrication.
Suns rise and set; beasts mate, birds migrate in due season;
And, in the desert, a sandstone monolith's erosion
Is an aeon-glass.

We fashion calendars and clocks to reckon
How time is naturally spent, but nothing
In nature specifies millennia. History
Is our invention.

A silver wedding anniversary; fifty years
Since VE and VJ Day; the centenary
Of poet, painter, or musician; a decade designated
This or that.

We need, it's clear, to find in secularity
Some human meaning. As for the Year 2000,
It will serve as well as any to signify redemption
In God's own time.

NATIVITY

*for Emily Song, born in China, adopted and brought to the U. S.*
*when one year old by our daughter Meg and her husband Steve*

Christmas nears, as we, here in Wales,
Impatient as your foster-parents
Preparing a home in Brooklyn,
Await your advent. Translated
From East to West, transplanted
As ignorant still, as innocent,
Of such distinctions as when
You entered our world, wailing,
Reaching blindly for love's embrace.

No more, no less a stranger
Than, at their moment of birth,
All of our children, and welcome
As our dear child, dear grandchild,
You are being reborn, becoming,
Through a prolonged gestation,
Part of the family.

Where will we be when you read this?
Still here in Wales? Translated
From space and time—to nowhere?
To the home, Love's eternal heart,
Our earthly homes foreshadow?

Never mind. Love is what matters.
The love that at this season
Reaches out in anticipation,
Annihilating time and space, embracing
This latest grandchild's coming,
Will be there, our love incarnate,
With you, and all our children,
At the heart of the family.

# CHILDERMASS
*28 December 1996*

In the Christian calendar, there's little time
To linger in the sentiments of Christmas.
Although behind the altar rail the Child
Still smiles within the creche,
We are called now to recollect the day
His surrogates were slaughtered.

And we recall, this year, Dunblane.
Like bread and wine, we bring those innocents to the altar.
Last March, as we watched and listened, in our minds
Were Ben in Houston, just turned six,
Emma in Sydney, almost seven.
Today, we said, the Wolf
Ate Red Riding Hood and loped back to the forest,
The Baby Bear had Goldilocks for lunch,
The Wicked Queen put Beauty
To sleep forever. After this,
How can we tell our grandchildren stories
With happy endings?

And yet, the calendar insists, we must.
The year has just begun. The darkest day
Is still to come, and Easter.
Beyond the creche the cross assumes
The Child within the fractured flesh of God,
And the host uplifted, broken,
Calls us to celebrate, uncomprehending,
How in the shattered bodies of the children
He died for good.

# UNTIMELY

Too warm for January. All through town
Front gardens blaze with daffodils—no biding
Time till Saint David's Day. Though as to that,
Their greenhouse blooms unfurl each week in florist shops.

And hot cross buns turned up today in Safeway.
*Post-Christmas fare*, the PR person says.
You'll find them any time in Marks and Spencer.
A *luxury version*'s on the shelves this year.

If Nature, as it seems, can disregard
Its proper rhythms, why not us? But still,
We'll wait to purchase daffodils until
Gŵyl Ddewi, eat our hot cross buns in Lent.

We'll sing no carols before Advent's over.
We'll leave our tree untrimmed till Christmas Eve.
We need to punctuate our ordinary time
With observation of a day, a season.

# EPITHALAMION IN AUTUMN

*for our grand-daughter Hannah Beth Shales and Patrick Marcotti,*
*married 3 October 1998 in Ogunquit, Maine*

Yours are the starring roles, but we,
Grandparents, visible history,
The past impersoned, autumnal presence
At this October wedding,
Have our part in, fact not fiction,
Your production, sacred act
Of mutual self-surrender.

Our fifty incredible wedded
Years affirm, like the turning leaves,
The significance of seasons.
Here and now must become
There and then, and the love you vow
Will change. Timeless Love requires
The selves we live to invent
Themselves in tenses, embody
Love anew with each day's birth.
This rite, more than you can know,
Is an act not solely of love,
Act of faith, act of hope,
As you step, hand in hand, bright-faced,
Lightly in time, and enter
The mystery of marriage.

Begin, now and here, with our
Ancestral blessing. May timeless Love
Lighten your darkest times, and grace
The selves you become together,
Joy deepening, as you embrace
Love incarnate in every season.

# THE GIFT

You were late coming back today. After an hour,
I stood at the window waiting, angry, afraid,
Like a child who's lost his mother in a crowded shop.

Separation anxiety. Over-dependence.
Call it what one will, whenever you are out
The lack of you pervades our living room.

No need to be sorry. Be however late you must,
So long as you come back. Such moments are a blessing,
Mementos of our ultimate disjunction.

I take you for granted. The air I breathe,
Heedless; the ground beneath my thoughtless feet.
The love I'm daily given, undeserving.

Forgive me that it takes your absence to remind me
How you grace a world where nothing else
Can be taken for granted.

## II.   A Change of Sky

*A HOME AWAY*

*(for David and Marianne, Erin and Maggie and Emma)*

*You are in the spaces*
*Between the poems. Your three-year home*
*Was our home base,*
*A place of ordinary restful days*
*After tourist expeditions.*

*Quite unlike your house*
*On Long Island. Small lizards soaked up sun*
*On the boles of palms*
*As we sat beside the pool, and a possum*
*Scrabbled on the roof at night.*

*But the rooms brimmed*
*With familiar voices, family noises,*
*Birthday celebrations,*
*And the silent comfort in a foreign land*
*Of welcome, and love, and home.*

# TOURISTS

Natural, the plaint that visitors by visiting
Spoil what they visit for. We change a place
By entering. It enters us, and changes.

This too is natural, the hankering for elsewhere:
We leaf through brochures, scan the travel shows,
And spin the globe's kaleidoscope. We step

Outside our ordinary time, invent
The luxury of being transient, duty-free
Observers underneath a foreign sky.

Strangeness like beauty's in the eye
Of the beholder. Naive our gaze—the native's
Commonplace is our exotic. We must read

The text without the context; complexity
Gets lost in our translation. Never mind.
Redefined by otherness, refreshed

By differentiation, we return
As strangers. We re-enter
Our common places. They enter us, and change.

# IN TRANSIT

Some turn their watches to the time in Sydney.
Some leave untampered with
The London time we've left. Upon the screen,
Film after film,
Sitcom after sitcom, flitting
Metamorphoses of space and time.

We do not care what hour it is in Bangkok.
The flight attendant
Informs us anyway. A walkabout inside
The airport limbo,
And we are sealed once more within
This capsule that transmutes our common day.

Godlike the facile play with times and places
Upon the screen,
Beyond the windows. Unserious the interim
Of watching, chatting,
Eating, dozing. It takes a touch
Of turbulence to bring us down to earth.

# INITIATION

Fast-forwarded, from a cold and rainy
Wednesday night,
Into a warm and sunny Friday morning,

Our bodies keep
Aberystwyth time. We wake to a raucous
Aussie chorus,

Lorikeets wailing like angry babies,
Serenading
Dawn with siren and slide-whistle.

April, and we walk
On autumn leaves, familiar reds and yellows,
Through streets where palm-trees

Flourish, cockatoos skim gum-trees, clumps
Of sunlit snow,
And this bush we pass is putting forth

A bird-of-paradise.
The shopping mall looks thoroughly American:
Supermarket,

Drugstore and deli, bakery and bank.
The paper dollars
Are parrot-hued, flimsy. Evaporate

As swiftly as the cockatoos.

# VIEWS OF THE SYDNEY OPERA HOUSE

Inescapable apparition, unignorable
      In Harbour, on postcard racks,
    Great wind-swollen concrete sails.

Irresistible tourist attraction, blank
      Insect eyes, heavy-lidded,
    Unblinking at our lenses.

Shark fins, enormous moth wings, helmets
      Of intergalactic raiders,
    Architectural aberration.

Post-modernist fossil, spines of a de-
      Constructed stegosaurus,
    Monstrous multiplex mollusc.

Excrescence, extrusion, photogenic from any angle,
      It signifies Sydney.
    Cardiff Bay should be so lucky.

## AT WARATAH PARK

In the scruffy bushland paddock
We are feeding the kangaroos.
Small and grey, greedy,
They submit to the children's petting.
The emus, more aloof,
Stay near the fences, stalking,
Now and then condescending
To take bread at our hands.
One languid kangaroo
Lolls in the autumn sunshine.

Suddenly they are moving,
All of them, away from us,
Hop past our outstretched palms,
All in the same direction.
And the emus race, stiff-legged,
All in the same direction.
The kangaroos sit, the emus
Stand, alert, unalarmed,
At one end of the paddock,
Gazing in the same direction.

Nothing there. Do they listen
To some ordinary sound
Beyond our human hearing?

A silent congregation,
Tense, senses attending
Something utterly beyond.

## EMU DREAMING

Long ago grounded, head high,
I soberly stride while flocks
Of featherbrains take the air.

I am double-glazed, well-tempered
In the desert blaze and freeze.
Down to earth father, I brood
Her clutch of green eggs, and rear
Our chicks myself. I process
Poisonous berries, and seed
Soil for another harvest.

Why then why should I envy
Budgerigars and finches
Their lightweight lifestyles?
I stand on my dignity.

   ★  ★  ★

They're big! So big it puts a strain
On one's ovipositor.

And green. Never did like green.
Not for eggs.

Laying them's left me limp.
I need a holiday.

He got what he wanted. Now
He can take the consequence.

## PLATYPUS DREAMING

I'm shy. You would be too
If every time they came to the zoo
People peered at you, and pointed,
And laughed at such a funny-looking thing.

Whatever, whoever created me knew
What he, she, or it was up to.
I was told to take to water, flatten
Into a streamlined body for swimming,

Sprout thick hair for insulation, web
My front paws into paddles, employ
My hind feet and tail as a rudder.
As for this bill you find so comical,

It's a food-detector. Eyes shut, and ears and nostrils,
I prospect for prey in sand and gravel,
Scoop it up, store it in the pouches of my cheeks,
And surface to munch on tasty crustaceans.

And what's so odd about laying eggs?
I sit, hugging two at a time, folded
Between my broad flat tail and belly,
And curl the snout you think is silly

To breathe on them warmly until they hatch
And suck milk from my hair. I teach my children
To frolic in streams, dive and hunt like me,
Rejoicing to be what they are.

Take a look at yourselves. Can you say,
After century on century,
That you have yet become the creature
You were meant to be?

## KOALA DREAMING

All at once some night, all across Australia,
We will bare our teeth, unsheathe our claws,
Clamber down from the eucalyptus boughs.

Fierce our teddy-bear faces as we amble,
Grey fur abristle, a march of marsupials,
From every zoo into suburb and city,

Crying out: "We have paid a high price for cuteness.
We have had enough of posing with the tourists,
Being cuddled by the kiddies, advertising Qantas.

Fellow-animals, give us back our animality!
We were made, like you, for ourselves, not you,
By whatever should be praised for our making.

Let us feed and brawl and breed in peace."

## ECHIDNA DREAMING

Out of the time before this insular continent
Cast off from the mainland,
I trundles towards you, twitching my elastic beak,
Shaking my spikes.

Evolutionary sidestep, experimental mammal,
I lays a single egg,
And I suckles the blind, naked hatchling
At a milk-patch in my pouch.

If threatened, I bristles at the mouth of a burrow,
Or I curls in a prickly ball;
When there's fire in the bush, I buries myself,
And I sprouts from the ashes.

To aborigines, I symbolizes death
And resurrection.
To you, could be I'm an emblem of survival—
Or of motherhood?

# AT THE OLGAS

1. *Minga*, the Anangu call us tourists. Ants.
   One line flows up the rocks. One trickles down.

   The heat, sharp stones, sore feet, the flies.
   I turn from the canyon mouth

   To see you sitting small below,
   Sensibly in shade. The flies, the flies.

   You are looking towards me, waving.
   I am, as I stumble back sweating,

   Not waving but swatting.

2. In 1872, our guidebook says, exploring the desert,
   Ernest Giles, when he sighted the tallest of these domes,
   Christened it Mount Olga,
   After the Queen of Wurtemmburg. The guidebook
   Doesn't tell us why.

   Two years before, at Mootwingee's caves,
   He carved the letter G
   To show that he'd been. He called the paintings there
   Weak endeavours of benighted beings'
   Darkened minds.

3. *Kata Tjuta*, the Anangu call them. Many Heads.
   If we catch a hint of faces on these skulls,
   They are not human. They keep another time,
   Care nothing for our naming.

   Gigantic headstones, relics
   Of an inland sea, a mountain range, the rivers
   That wore the mountains into gravel. Granite and basalt
   Pebbles, cobbles, boulders. Sand and mud
   Cemented them, a geological
   *Memento mori*.

# ULURU

1. Merely a rock. The visible tip
   Of a slab that stretches far below the ground.

   A sandstone monolith.
   Solidified sediment folded, faulted, tilted,
   Eroded by millennia of wind and rain,
   And rusted: grey arkose oxidized.

   There is water in the shallow caves, but it has
   No underground spring. Rain run-off
   Fashions the pot holes and the plunge pools.

   Light refracted by the atmosphere, reflected
   From the rock and clouds,
   Ruddies it at sunrise and at sunset.

   Upon the dunes around grow mulga and spinifex,
   Wattle and grevillea. The sand
   Is as it has been for thirty-thousand years.

   The rock
   Continues to erode.


2  In the Dreaming, the Anangu say,
   Kuniya camps and hunts beside a water-hole
   On a large flat sandhill. It turns to stone
   And becomes Uluru.

   In the Dreaming, one of the Anangu says,
   All the Liru men come from their homeland
   To spear a Kuniya. The holes in the rock
   Are from their spears. And the snake in this painting,
   That is the Kuniya man, speared.

At the women's site, Pulari,
At the men's, Warayuki,
Near the base of the rock,
Not far from the water-hole, Mutitjulu,
They know the singing and the rites,
They read the Ancestors' traces in the rock,
They see the tracks that bind Uluru to other sacred places
In the web of the Dreaming.

They keep its secrets.
To themselves, they are the People.
Their Dreaming is not ours.


3. Artificial oasis. Ayers Rock Resort
   Has low-level architecture: no building

   Is taller than the highest sand dune. Thick walls of masonry
   Insulate the buildings. Water

   Is pumped from underground bores, and then
   Desalinated. Waste water irrigates

   Green lawns and landscaped gardens.
   The Central Energy Plant

   Supplies hot water and air-conditioning.
   There are three hotels, and a Shopping Square

   With supermarket, tavern, bank, and gift shop,
   Travel agency and post office.

   Our hotel has a twenty-metre pool, a tennis court, three
                                                restaurants.
   Each room has a TV and a mini-bar.

   The walks are paved with bricks. Between the cracks,
   Tiny mounds of fine red sand, a to-and-fro of ants.

4. For us it is somewhere special to go, like Stonehenge or
                                                        Chartres,
   But a natural marvel, a huge single rock in the desert
   At the heart of the continent, ancient, something

   We did not make, that we can make of what we will.
   We ride in air-conditioned coaches to the designated spot
   Amid the spinifex, and wait, cameras at the ready,

   For sunset and the fluent shades of redness in the rock.
   Some of us bring folding chairs and tables, picnic baskets
   With biscuits, cheese, and wine. The desert air

   Is brimming with our babble: German, Japanese,
   English and American and native white Australian.
   A jet's white contrail scars the blue above.

   It begins. Our shadows lengthen as the cameras
   Whir and click until the sun is down
   Behind us, and the rock is dull. Our coaches

   Transport us coolly back to the resort.
   And in the early morning some will make the painful
   Climb to the top, while others do the six-mile circuit

   Of stations round the base. At the Makura Centre
   We will purchase a carving, or perhaps a painting on bark,
   An x-ray vision of emu, kangaroo, goanna.

   A souvenir. A work of art. A relic.


5. There is water here, where sunstruck air
   Illuminates  bare earth.

   It is a rock eroding in the desert.

   It is a mask of God.

45

# DOWN UNDER

Lifeless from one mile up the miles and miles
Of flat red sand, dull blobs of brown and green.
We overlook
The sap astir in spinifex and mulga,
The seeds, the seeds

That feed the pipit and the hopping mouse,
The blossoming of daisy and acacia,
The desert rose.
Somewhere down there a thorny devil feasts
On ants, on ants,

A bearded dragon stores up solar power,
A spotted frog has burrowed deep in mud.
Newly hatched,
The shield shrimp seize the day before their puddle dries
And mate, and mate.

Our plane's a speeding cloud whose shadow leaves
Untouched a world inscrutable to us
Below, below.
Life breeds, life feeds on life, indifferent to our passing
Above, above.

# DEEP NORTH

Here above the Tropic of Capricorn
We expected hotels
Would be built to keep the rainforest out.

But we grope from room to restaurant
Along a twisting trail,
Under a canopy of leaves as thick

As on the Atherton Tableland, and past
A shadowed lagoon—
Are those bathers, or crocodiles?

A cloudburst punctuates dinner,
And we must dash back
To our room beneath dripping branches.

Here the natural is perverse, part
Of the artifice.
Better, like the aborigines,

To know one's proper place in nature,
Or else see to it
That nature knows its proper place.

# CANE TOAD DREAMING

We didn't ask to come. You brought us to Queensland
From Hawaii to wipe out the sugar cane beetle.
Serves you right

That the beetles proliferated. As did we: you find us
Squatting on paths, in gardens and driveways,
A proper menace

To your dogs and children, squirting our venom
If they get too close. You can stun us by shining
A torch in our eyes,

Pop us into plastic bags, fill up your buckets,
Shove us in a freezer to hibernate forever,
But dead we are still

Good for nothing, not even compost. The only one
Who could love a cane toad is another cane toad,
Though maybe not:

Lust isn't love, and what more can you expect
Of a cane toad? God, you'll concede, must
Love us, although

God knows what He was thinking of when He evolved us.
Maybe a proof, if you need it, that the world
Wasn't made just for you.

# BUNGY JUMPING AT KURANDA

1. Reeled up slowly, up from the thick green
   Screen of foliage, up
   To the top of the yellow crane,

   She steps from the basket, pauses, poses,
   Overlooking
   The canvas roofs of the Rainforest Market,

   And us, arrested on the hillside,
   Looking on.

2. Done for fun. Would they understand, I wonder,
   This toying with terror, the men
   Who hacked roadbed up the mountain,
   Laid track that hugs the cliffs,

   Hung with fingertips to the workface, dropped
   Down, down the unruffled
   Throat of the gorge?

3. She is poised on the edge of the platform.
   Lifts arms overhead, spreads them wide.
   Bends, tilts her body forwards.

   I cannot look. I could not look
   As the floor of the gorge subsided, dwindled below
   Bridge after bridge, and empty air
   Compelled towards the train's open window.

   One hand clasped by yours, firmly, the other
   Clenching the armrest, I
   Kept eyes left on the bankside
   And welcomed every tunnel.

4.  I see her falling slowly, smiling,
    Sailing joyously down
    Through the void above the market, past
    My onlooker's shuttered eyes.

    Always an onlooker. Non-
    Participant, observer,
    Even of my own life. When did I ever
    Surrender like that, trusting
    Myself to providence?

    Once, perhaps. Once only.
    And even then, as we vowed,
    You took the greater risk.

5.  The ankle harness, you tell me,
    Holds. We watch as her body
    Bounces and swings, a doll dangled
    Upside down from a gallows,
    Till it's lowered out of sight.

    Once at least. Once for certain,
    I must let go or be pushed,
    Drop into emptiness. Will that moment
    Numb me with its horror,
    Or astonish me with joy?

    Be there, love, oh be there,
    Wherever you may be,
    A hand to hold mine firmly
    As I fall into the dark.

# AT MOORE'S REEF

We peer through the transparent side of the semi-
                                        submersible
At toys for a baby's bathtub. Crimson, bright blue, clown-
                                        striped,
Squares and rectangles, seemingly fashioned of plastic.
                    Fish
Shouldn't look like this. They ought to be properly fish-
                                        shaped
And soberly sided, not primped out in purples and yellows,
A po-faced gaudy parade flaunting flippantly past our
                                        window.

Never mind what the ichthyologists or David
Attenborough
Have to say about evolution and adaptation.
This spectacle shakes any faith we have had in Nature.
                    God
Is the only sensible explanation for such an explosion
Of implausible forms and colours, this riotous
Joke, this divine extravaganza, this joy, this wonder.

## CORAL DREAMING

I are we. We am I.
Animal, but you cannot
Keep me as a pet, look us in the eye.
Snorkel around if you will,
I has nothing to do with you.

More plant than animal, more rock than anything,
Blips of polyps, I lives within
The fans and fronds, the cups and horns,
Of our skeleton garden.

Garden? A jungle. Soft I's and hard
Contend for turf. Parrots
Nip nip nip
Bits of us away. Crowns of thorns
Suck me wet and hollow.

We is home to butterflies, clowns, and bats,
Horses and dragons,
Jewels, damsels, and porcupines.
Nudibranchs nuzzle my branches.
Stars feather our labyrinth.
Angels flirt through my latticework.

We stay put. I bud our clones
Into colonies of me. But on
A soft night in spring, when the waters are still,
And the signal comes over the internet,
I explode through undersea moons.
We eject myselves in clouds of balloons,
Pink and red, blue and orange and green,
And I end as I always begin.

Your millennia mean
Nothing to us. We am what I are
For aeons of now.

# HERITAGE

Their living-room's black-specked yellow walls,
They tell us proudly,
Are made of convict bricks. His ancestor
Sailed down under as an officer, hers
Was fettered below decks.
1788, First Fleet. First families
Of a nation founded as a dumping ground.

We dine at *The Italian Village*, after strolling
The Quay and The Rocks,
Window-shopping the boutiques and galleries
Where pent between grey-green bush and vacant sea
Involuntary exiles
Blunted their picks and spades on virgin soil,
Spread seed, and hand-cut stone, and starved in makeshift
huts.

In Old Sydney Town, an hour or so to the north
Along the Freeway,
They play at pioneering, dressing up as
Redcoats and convicts. A tavern and a schoolroom,
Bullocks and waggons,
A shearing-shed, a smithy, and a windmill.
The English flag, each morning and each evening,

Is raised and lowered, and the cannon fired.
Each day ends
With a convict wedding. At intervals,
There are trials and floggings. Pure make-believe.
No blood is shed,
No flesh is spattered on the crowd, no backs
Are shredded to the bone for petty crimes.

History, like the restoration of The Rocks,
As tourist attraction.
And yet, however scrubbed and artificial,
Acknowledgement and celebration of beginnings,
Act of homage
To those reluctant voyagers whose graves
First made of alien earth a fertile homeland.

INTERLUDE
*The Chinese Gardens at Darling Harbour*

Sydney's not as frenetic as New York or London,
But hardly restful. Traffic

Keeps the Harbour brisk with ferry and jet cat,
And the Marketplace

Is a racket of shops and food courts. Here, however,
There's an unforeseen asylum,

A tranquil labyrinth where shopper and tourist
Stroll slowly from

Pavilion to pavilion, pause to consider
Two amiable dragons,

Blue and gold, delighting in a pearl that floats
On pacific waves.

Cunning artifice, Oriental sanctum,
Unwinding us easily

By lake and waterfall, loquat and lotus,
Rock and bamboo,

Into an eternity of contemplation,
Till it's time for tea.

# EUCALYPT

It makes the most of its land.
When Australia sailed into isolation,
As rainforest dwindled it picked up sticks
And colonized the continent.

It cultivates diversity.
It is red gums and grey.
It soars as mountain ash. It twists
Stems into shrubs of mallee.

It sustains mistletoe.
It shelters rosellas. It entertains
Kookaburras' laughter.
It cuddles koalas.

It satisfies the sweet tooth of gliders.
On its limelit floor
The lyrebird stages
His song and dance.

It plays with fire. When lightning sets
Leaf oils ablaze, beneath charred bark
Leaf buds quicken. It robes its blackened
Skeleton in green.

# ST. MARY'S CATHEDRAL, SYDNEY

It faces north, not east. Two statues,
Green in their pedestalled glory, flank
The steps to the south entry.
Not saints, we discover—a cardinal and an archbishop,
Whatever we're to think of that.

Within, the Chapel of the Irish Saints
Is a puzzle too. One window
Portrays Augustine's mission to the English,
A second honours Newman. There's room in the third
For Saint Patrick and Saint Brendan.

Australia has, so far, a single
Official saint. Or saint-to-be: Blessed Mary McKillop,
Once excommunicated by a bishop.
There are books on her in the cathedral shop,
But in the church itself, no recognition.

She has, it's true, her own museum in North Sydney,
With tomb and chapel,
A coffee shop, and an exuberant
Aboriginal painting. A homelier place
Than the cathedral.

This massive fabric bears its witness, though,
With three Rose Windows,
West for Adam, east for Jesus, south for Peter,
And on the western wall a convict priest
Says Mass in a colonist's kitchen.

Heads of saints
Adorn the sandstone columns. Mary
Is crowned in the great north window.
The opulent high altar's sculpture
Depicts the Last Supper and the Crucifixion.

If too much in this cathedral
Embarrasses with riches, seems
Too much a celebration of itself, an idol edifice,
It is nonetheless
An incarnation of our Dreaming:

Bound within the Gospel songlines, binding us
To other sacred places, here
Is God, tormented and despised,
Dying without dignity,
A poor man raised to be a saving presence
In bread and wine, in flesh and blood.

# PACKING

In they go, the booklets, postcards, snapshots
From Sydney, Ayers Rock, Cairns.

But what of these, the brochures for the places
We didn't get to? The opal mine in Coober Pedy,

Ballarat, the goldfields of Kalgoorlie,
The high rises of Perth, the Bungle Bungle ranges,

Kimberley's gorges, Katherine, Kakadu,
The Pinnacles' fossil forest, Canberra's Parliament House.

Tasmania remains a name. Its devil
Sneered as we passed in the Taronga Zoo.

All that we saw of Alice Springs was airport.
Untravelled on by us, the Melbourne trams.

We haven't tasted wine in Hunter Valley,
Surfed on the Gold Coast, swum at Bondi Beach—

Nor wanted to. We almost took a train to the Blue Mountains,
Then spent the day in Sydney on a bus.

Our time and stamina and budget have their limits.
Most of Australia's outback still to us.

No matter. We have overflown the never-never, drifted
On a rainforest river, rocked and rolled

In a cat through the Coral Sea. In our sixties,
Four weeks of the exotic is enough.

Pack all the brochures, though. You never know,
We might be coming back. And should we not,

It does no harm to contemplate, without regret,
A world of places where we haven't been.

# SOUVENIR

At Sydney Airport, opposite the Duty Free,
Still another shop
With aboriginal artefacts. We are taking back
A little box of coasters packed with Dreamings:
Crocodile, Goanna, Emu, Jabiru, Fish.

Their paintings were everywhere, like the cafe signs that
                                         promised
Devonshire Teas,
But of themselves, in our few tourist weeks,
We have seen little. Performers in body paint
At the restaurant in Kuranda, the shapeless woman

Shouting to no one in the Ayers Rock parking lot,
That token native
Didgeridoodling at Old Sydney Town.
And in the papers, athletes, protest movements,
Speakers at a Cultural Diversity Conference in Sydney.

They are the aliens now. Our Dreaming is not theirs.
For Americans,
A sorry shadow of our history. Manifest Destiny.
Cheap grace, this retrospective guilt,
Knowing we would have dealt with them no better.

We bring them with us, bright dots, cross-hatchings, stick
                                         figures,
Tucked in our luggage,
Taking off from a sunny autumn afternoon
To land in spring, on a chill grey London morning,
An overnight rewinding through the looking-glass.

# AFTERWORDS

Dear fellow-traveller, your photographs,
Invisible behind, within, these poems,
Reminders, revelations, catalysts,
Maintain the fiction of their present tense.

Now, in this humdrum summer back in Wales,
That holiday's prehistory, a Dreaming,
Stored with the other stories that sustain
Our sojourn in the country of old age.

No choice. No maps, no brochures. Each day's landscape
Is familiar, strange. Each night's a candid warning
This journey is our last. Today, at least,
We'll travel joyfully together, thankful

For the timeliness of marriage, guarded, guided
By the timelessness of Love.

# III. UNSELVING

*for those who suffer, and those who care*

*You cannot take itself*
*From any human soul*
                    Emily Dickinson, #1351


*I think I am a verb instead of a personal pronoun. A verb*
*is anything that signifies to be; to do; or to suffer. I*
*signify*
    *all these.*

                    Ulysses S. Grant, dying, to his physician


*What? shall we receive good at the hands of God, and*
*shall we not receive evil?*
                    Job 2, 10

First Sunday after Trinity. Three years retired,
They stroll down to the seafront after church.
They watch the marbled influx of the tide,
The sunlit swoopings of the terns and gulls,
The pigeons strutting on the prom, decide
Upon a restaurant for lunch. An ordinary couple,
Making the most of ordinary time.

She pauses in mid-sentence, open-mouthed,
Eyes empty. Then: Getting old, I guess.
I don't know what I was about to say. Nothing
Important, anyway.
                 Never mind, he says,
It will come back.

They leave the restaurant, stroll home,
Read the Sunday paper, nap. They wake to make
A lazy love till supper time and television.

He will remember this as the beginning.

           ★    ★    ★

Behind the eyes, beneath the hair, below
The bone: grey spongy hemispheres.
Intricate electric interlacings.
Axons, synapses, dendrites. Wetware
Fabricates the world in its reflexive loom.

Stutters in the shuttles. Silicon
Compounds with aluminium in the cortex.
Nerve ends
Thicken into plaques. Pairs of filaments
Spiral round one another in the neurons.
Tangles fret the networks—break the codes.

           ★    ★    ★

What about Crete, he says.
You liked it there. Or Malta?
All those foreigners, she says.

York then, he says. Or Scotland.
A little holiday
Would do us both some good.

Later perhaps, she says. And don't
Keep going on about it. I'm
Not up to it right now.

      ★     ★     ★

Silly, she says. So silly. I got lost.
He has waited
In front of Woolworth's for an hour,

Bored, impatient, fearful,
For her to find a way
Through familiar streets.

      ★     ★     ★

That isn't like you, love, he says.
She has forgotten
To send their daughter's birthday card.

Serves her right, she says. She never
Phones us or writes.
                 She called
Only last week. Remember?

Did she ? Never mind.
It doesn't really matter.
She won't care.

      ★     ★     ★

She gives him wine and sandwiches for breakfast.
She leaves the water running in the tub.

The teapot's in the bedroom wardrobe.
The groceries are in the oven.

Her coat's on
Inside out.

★   ★   ★

He wakes to find the bed
Half empty. She has gone

Past midnight, in her nightgown,
Four streets and eighteen years astray.

A policeman brings her home.
He leads her back to bed.

He holds her, sobbing, till she sleeps.

★   ★   ★

Blood tests. Urine tests.
CAT scan. PET scan.

How old are you, the doctor asks.
What day is it? What month? What year?

Where do you live? Where are you? Who
Is Prime Minister?

Black shoes. Red car. Two hundred Talbot Street.
Repeat, and memorize.
Black shoes. Red car. Two hundred Talbot Street.

Spell world, the doctor tells her. Now
Spell it backwards. Now

Spell home. Spell it
Backwards.

Count down, the doctor says. From one hundred.
Ninety-five. Ninety. Ninety.

Red, she says. Red Talbot.

★   ★   ★

Prognosis: devolution. From knife and fork
To spoon. From spoon to fingers.

Slow erosion. Loss
Of definition. Deconstruction.

Sentences to phrases. Phrases
To words. Slurred syllables.

★   ★   ★

He takes the Lord's name

Christ
Christ
Christ

a curse

Jesus
Jesus
Jesus

a prayer

Christ
Christ
Christ

in vain.

★     ★     ★

Forty years younger, she awoke this morning
In the first year of their marriage. Burnt
The eggs and bacon. Wept.

They sit together on the sofa. She
Turns the pages of the photo album.
Faces. Places. He
Recalls, reminds. The London flat.
A holiday in Cornwall. Friends.
Themselves at thirty-one.
Their daughter's graduation.

He retrieves the moments, reconstructs
Shared history. Pages
Age them in turning. He restores
The storied self beside him, wanting
No other, younger wife.

★     ★     ★

A good day, he says. She nods and smiles.
They have been to the library, shopped,
Had lunch in town. Spent the day
Together. Like your old self, he says.

★     ★     ★

Stop, she says, and pulls away,
Her voice a girl's. In the bedroom dusk
Her vague face is as young as in the photos.

It's wrong, she says. My mother
Told me it's wrong. You mustn't
Touch me there.

★    ★    ★

The house is hostile. Doors
Gape stupidly. She stops, lost

Between the bedroom and the bathroom,
Crying to go home.

★    ★    ★

Not, she says. You're not
My daughter. Nothing like
My daughter. My daughter's
Young. And beautiful, not
Anything like you.

★    ★    ★

These words. They spill from her.
He is bewildered. So is she.

He didn't know she knew these words.
She doesn't know them.

She isn't speaking them.
They speak themselves.

★    ★    ★

Where they would go together, now
He takes her along, to shops, to church, ignoring
The stares and whispers. She

Is his care, his child, his love.
Wife to him only when she sleeps.

★　　★　　★

Two days a week he leaves her
At the Day Care Centre, as he once
Delivered their daughter to her nursery school

For games and songs. A guilty getaway.
He wanders about town, stops in
At library or video shop, walks the prom

And contemplates the tide's indifference. At the Centre
She sulks and quarrels, frets and whines.
No graduation. After three weeks

A Day Care Centre dropout.

★　　★　　★

This room is wrong, she says. All wrong.
The door's
In the wrong wall. My rocking-chair,
It should be by the window.

This wall is wrong. The colour's
Wrong. Why
Is it all so wrong?

Where have you brought me? Home?
This isn't home. Not any
Home of mine.

★　　★　　★

71

Familiar rituals. A happy Christmas.
Tree-trimming. carol service, creche.
Remember, says the preacher, that this Child
Took flesh to die for us.

She knows her grandson. They
Watch a Disney film together, play
Two games of Snakes-and-Ladders.

She nods off in her chair. Better,
Their daughter whispers. She's
Getting better. Isn't she?

★     ★     ★

Get out, she says. Get out. What
Are you doing here? I don't

Know you. Get out. My husband
Will be back any minute. He'll

Deal with you. You'll see.

★     ★     ★

Thing, she says. Thing. For everything.
That thing she's looking at.
This thing she's holding.

The words abandon her. The world rebels.
She cannot find the names to make things know
Their proper place.

★     ★     ★

Eyes closed, she sits with hands on knees.
The doctor lightly strokes one knee, one hand.

72

Which cheek, he asks. Which hand?
This one. No, this. Again. And then again,

Eyes open. This one. Again. No, this.

★    ★    ★

Tonight the TV's an aquarium.
In ocean depths bright blips of fish.

Polyps unfurl from limestone skeletons.
At low tide in the rockpools: brittlestars,
Seaslugs, fan worms, limpets, spider crabs.

Arms writhe. Legs scuttle.
Feed and spawn and die.

Purposeless process. He cannot
Humanize this world. He cannot glimpse
A God within its making and unmaking.
He cannot bear
To stare into its mirror.

She cries out from the bedroom.
He turns the television off.

★    ★    ★

*Dance Band Days*. Ray Noble plays
'The Way You Look Tonight'.

He bows, and helps her stand.
He holds her firmly, guides

Her shuffling steps around the living room.
She hums the tune.

★    ★    ★

Wife-sitters, now and then,
Release him for an hour to himself.
Relief. A joyless freedom. A desertion.

Next-door-but-one comes often.
Never a friend. A boring man.
Good neighbour.

*     *     *

What's happening, she says.
She rocks and stares and sighs.

Flowers on the windowsill
Wilt in their vase. That's me, she says.

He wheels her to the prom. They stop to watch
The flush of sunset ebb into the bay.

Yes, she says. Oh yes. And smiles.

*     *     *

The labour's undivided. He cooks and washes up,
Hoovers and launders. Takes some pride
In mastering these mysteries.

*     *     *

They sing 'Amazing Grace' on *Songs of Praise*.
Lost and found. Blind and see.

She remembers the words.
Joyful, she sings along.

He joins in. Questions silently.

*     *     *

74

Five minutes, and his angry words
Are unremembered. No need
To ask forgiveness. No way
To be forgiven, heal the separation
In love's conjunction.

★   ★   ★

The silences are empty. Once
They floated in the stillnesses that brimmed
Their living room.

No need for talk. He would read.
She would write letters, or crochet.

A glance across from time to time.
A smile.

★   ★   ★

He could not bear a universe
As empty as her eyes. He needs
Someone to pray to. Someone to blame.

Above their bed, the crucifix.
The nail-pierced God-forsaken
Someone God became

In emptying Himself.

★   ★   ★

Cartesian at such moments, he can watch
Himself undress her, stuff
Soiled clothing in the laundry basket,
Unflinching at the stench,

75

Observe, amused, the naked man
Who leads her naked to the shower,
Soaps and rinses breasts and crotch and buttocks
Passive beneath his hands.

Dispassionate, he dries and powders
Drooping flesh. Will not remember when
Their nakedness was never casual,
Its privacy a joyous revelation.

★   ★   ★

Sorry, his daughter says. I'm sorry.
Sitting all day, and seeing her
Like this, it's like

A wake without the burial. I
Can't take it. Won't. I won't
Remember her like this.

That's not my mother there. My mother's
Gone. That isn't
Anyone I know.

★   ★   ★

Bereaved, unwived. Only she
Has seen his private face, heard
His private voice.

Unmanned, unmade. He cannot find
Himself within her inexpressive words,
Her unreflecting eyes.

★   ★   ★

He reads only light romances.
Rosamund Pilcher. Elizabeth Cadell.
Or Wodehouse farces, the absurdity
Of tangled plots incredibly
And happily resolved. He requires
Happy endings.

No escape. A hope
That comic fictions figure
Hope hereafter.

★   ★   ★

He is called to selfless loving, mindless
Of indifference or ignorance.

Atonement. Recompense.
Her love had always been
Less selfish than his own.

He must be to her
The mother love of God.
Providence.

★   ★   ★

There this morning, for a moment, back
Within her eyes.
Bewildered. Terrified.

She looked out and she knew him for a moment.
She almost spoke. Then disappeared
Behind her eyes.

As though, lost in twisting corridors,
She'd happened on a window. Tried
To open it. Turned away.

★   ★   ★

His prayers, when he can pray, are brief.
Lighten our darkness. Into your hands.

He does not question what he means, for fear
His prayers are for her death.

Let me, he prays, not grudge the caring.
Let each action be a prayer.

Keep me sound in mind and body.
Let me live for her.

★　　★　　★

Passed on, he's heard them say. Passed over.
Easier, perhaps, to think
That someone's elsewhere when they die
Than to believe in her existence now.

He lives by faith, the wife he loves
Invisible as God.

★　　★　　★

Intensive Care. He has surrendered her
To the professionals.

No suffering. What she is, she is.
Her body, tube-sustained,

Breathes artificial air. Each day
He visits it as though

He worshipped at a shrine. He strokes for hours
The fragile unresponding fingers.

He kisses them in leaving.

★　　★　　★

They offer comfort, calling death
A merciful release. For her. For him.

How to answer? He is at a loss.
He lacks all purpose now.

Selfless. He cannot tell them
He lost himself in her.

★    ★    ★

Coffined, her selfless flesh
Was an empty tomb.

It was her absence that he buried.
He has not visited the grave.

She is with him again
In the living room silence.

She kneels beside him Sundays.
She prays with him at night.

She strolls with him
Along the prom.

She answers when he speaks
Of trivial things.

She will, he can believe,
Be present to the end.

Hereafter? He is content to leave hereafter
In the hands of God.

## NOTES & ACKNOWLEDGEMENTS

At Gettysburg. The site of a major battle that was a turning point in the U. S. Civil War. President Abraham Lincoln's famous address was delivered at the dedication of the cemetery on 19 November 1863.

Christmas Market, Lincoln. The closing lines refer to a sculpture on exhibit in the cathedral in December 1993.

Towards the Millennium. C. E. for 'Common Era' and B. C. E. for 'Before the Common Era' have come into increasing use by historians and others, particularly in the United States, as politically correct replacements for A. D. and B. C.

Childermass. The ancient English name for the Feast of the Holy Innocents, commemorating the children slain by Herod's soldiers (Matthew 2, 16). On 13 March 1996, 16 young children and their teacher were murdered at the primary school in Dunblane, Scotland, by Thomas Hamilton, who then shot himself.

A CHANGE OF SKY. The Dreaming is a term used by Australian aborigines in referring to their creation myths and to the ultimate reality that continues to sustain the earth and its creatures. Aboriginal artists often call their paintings 'dreamings', and I have borrowed the title for poems in which birds and animals are imagined as speaking to us out of their otherness. For information used in this sequence of poems I am indebted to John van den Beld's *Nature of Australia*, Wally Caruana's *Aboriginal Art*, and Robert Hughes' *The Fatal Shore*, and for one way to dispose of cane toads to an editorial in the *Barung Landcare Newsletter*.

UNSELVING. For information on Alzheimer's Disease, including representative case histories, I have consulted Donna Cohen and Carl Eisdorfer's *The Loss of Self* and Isabelle Gidley and Richard Shears' *We Never Said Goodbye*.

'Unselving' was first runner-up in *Stand*'s 1996 international poetry competition, and an abridged version was published in the magazine. 'Heron Music' was one of four runners-up in the Dulwich Festival poetry competition for 1996 and published in the competition anthology.

'Souvenir' was included in the PHRAS anthology for 1996. Other poems have previously appeared in *Acumen*, *The Interpreter's House*, *The New Welsh Review*, *Planet*, *Poems from Aberystwyth IX* and *X*, *Poetry Life*, *Poetry Wales*, *Scintilla*, *The Source*, and *The Western Mail*.

Joseph P. Clancy was born in 1928 in New York City, where he lived until he retired from teaching in 1990 and settled in Wales. He holds his Ph.D. from Fordham University and is Marymount Manhattan College's Emeritus Professor of English Literature and Theatre Arts.

His selected poems, *The Significance of Flesh*, had its U.K. publication in 1984, and a subsequent collection, *Here & There*, in 1994. He has translated extensively from Welsh literature—most recently the short stories of Kate Roberts; the poems of Saunders Lewis; a collection of folk poems, *Where There's Love*; and *The Light in the Gloom*, poems and essays by Alun Llywelyn-Williams—and with his wife Gertrude co-authored a mystery novel, *Death Is A Pilgrim: A Canterbury Tale*, featuring Geoffrey Chaucer as detective.

He is a Fellow of the English-Language Section of Yr Academi Gymreig (The Welsh Academy) and an Honorary Fellow of the University of Wales, Aberystwyth. He has been awarded an honorary D. Litt. by the University of Wales for his work as poet and translator.